SCIENCE EXPERIMENTS
Go Green

Om KIDZ
An imprint of Om Books International

First Published in 2023 by

Om KIDZ | Om Books International

Corporate & Editorial Office
A-12, Sector 64, Noida 201 301
Uttar Pradesh, India
Phone: +91 120 477 4100
Email: editorial@ombooks.com
Website: www.ombooksinternational.com

Sales Office
107, Ansari Road, Darya Ganj
New Delhi 110 002, India
Phone: +91 11 4000 9000
Email: sales@ombooks.com
Website: www.ombooks.com

ISBN: 978-93-52763-11-5

Printed in India

10 9 8 7 6 5 4 3 2 1

CONTENTS

Duration of Experiment

5 mins

This icon indicates approximately how long the experiment will take, including the set-up time.

Difficulty Level

The black bars in this icon indicate level of difficulty in doing this experiment with one icon depicting the least level of difficulty.

Adult Supervision

This icon indicates that parental supervision is required. Always have an adult beside you.

NOTE: All activities and experiments described in this book should be ideally performed with adult supervision. Parents and guardians are advised to oversee the children and assist them with any difficult or potentially harmful tools. Common sense and discretion are advised. The publisher does not assume any responsibility for any injuries or damages arising from any activities.

Tsp - teaspoon Tbsp - tablespoon ml - millilitre l - litre gm - gram 1 cup - 250 millilitre cm - centimetre

Potato Well

Duration of Experiment: 20 mins.

Difficulty Level:

What you need:

Knife

1 tsp sugar

2 potatoes

Dish

Water

What to do:

Step 1. Boil one potato.

Step 2. Slice off the top and bottom of both potatoes and scoop a hollow in each.

Step 3. Peel the lower half of each potato.

Step 4. Place the sugar in the hollow of each potato.

Step 5. Fill a dish with water and put both potatoes in it.

Step 6. Check the dish after 24 hours.

Step 7. The sugar in the boiled potato will remain the same but the sugar in the raw potato will be full of water.

SCIENCE AROUND US

Osmosis

In osmosis, liquids travel through a semi-permeable surface (like the potato skin). But potatoes aren't the only living things that can absorb water through their skin. Put your hand in water for 20 minutes and see what happens to your fingers!

What just happened? Water travels through the cell walls of living things. This process is called 'osmosis'. The cells in the boiled potato are dead, and so osmosis cannot take place.

Coloured Leaves

Duration of Experiment: 2 hours

Difficulty Level:

What you need:

Blotting paper

Glass jar

Spinach leaves

Acetone

What to do:

Step 1. Mash the spinach leaves into a pulp. Place the pulp at the bottom of the glass jar.

Step 2. Cover all the spinach with acetone.

Step 3. Suspend a strip of the blotting paper into the jar.

Step 4. In a few hours, you will be able to see various colours separating themselves on the blotting paper.

What just happened?

The acetone extracted the pigments from the leaves. This was absorbed by the blotting paper by a process called capillary action. The acetone evaporated and left the pigments behind.

Why Are Leaves Green

Duration of Experiment: 7 days

Difficulty Level:

What you need:

Scissors

Clips

Black chart paper

Plant

What to do:

Step 1. Cover a few leaves with black chart paper.

Step 2. Put the plant where it can get plenty of sunlight.

Step 3. After a week, take the black paper off. The leaves you had covered are not as green as the others.

What just happened?

Leaves get their green colour from a substance that they produce, called 'chlorophyll'. Chlorophyll can be made only in the presence of sunlight. The leaf wrapped in chart paper did not get any sunlight.

Grow a Plant

Duration of Experiment: 3 days

Difficulty Level:

What you need:

Sprouts

Cotton wool

Container

Water

What to do:

Step 1. Line the container with damp cotton.

Step 2. Place the sprouts on the damp cotton and leave it on a window sill.

Step 3. Every time the cotton dries up, dampen it again.

Step 4. The sprouts will grow in a few days.

What just happened?

You can see the sprout giving off small roots into the cotton, and a shoot begins to grow. Plants need water and sunlight to grow.

Graft a Plant

Duration of Experiment: 7 days

Difficulty Level:

What you need:

Craft knife

Potato plant

Tomato plant

String

Modelling clay

What to do:

Step 1. Pull the main stems of the potato and tomato plants together and tie them loosely with a string.

Step 2. Shave the bark till you can see the interior tubes.

Step 3. Tightly wrap string around the two shaved ends. Seal it with clay.

Step 4. After a week, cut off the old potato and old tomato plants above the wrapped part, creating a new 'pomato' plant.

What just happened?

The new plant imbibes properties of both the old plants. This process is called plant 'grafting'.

Smoky Prints

Duration of Experiment: 30 mins.

Difficulty Level:

What you need:

Leaf

Petroleum jelly

2 glass bottles

Gloves

Newspaper

Candle

! Be careful while heating the bottle. Fire can be dangerous.

What to do:

Step 1. Spread petroleum jelly on the bottle and heat it over a flame using a glove. Heat it till it is covered with soot.

Step 2. Roll the sooty bottle over the veins of the leaf.

Step 3. Place the leaf between two sheets of paper.

Step 4. Roll a clean bottle over the sheets. Turn the paper over.

What just happened?

Petroleum jelly is a product that is made up of carbon. On heating, this carbon forms soot.

Leafy Oxygen

Duration of Experiment: 2 hours

Difficulty Level:

What you need:

Seaweed

Glass jar

Water

What to do:

Step 1. Fill the jar with water.

Step 2. Put the seaweed in the jar.

Step 3. Place the jar in a room with bright sunshine.

Step 4. Watch the jar closely. You will notice air bubbles rising.

What just happened?

The air bubbles in the jar are oxygen. During the day, plants take in carbon dioxide and let out oxygen during photosynthesis.

Carrot Hanging

Duration of Experiment: 10 days

Difficulty Level:

What you need:

String

Knife

Long nail

Carrot

Water

What to do:

Step 1. Choose a carrot that has a few leaves on its head.

Step 2. Cut about two inches from the top.

Step 3. Take help from an adult to hollow out the carrot top.

Step 4. Push the nail in horizontally and tie the string to both the ends of the nail.

Step 5. Fill the hollow with water.

Step 6. Hang your carrot hanging with the leaves pointing downwards.

Step 7. Keep refilling the hollow every time it gets dry.

Step 8. Soon the leaves will start growing upwards against gravity.

SCIENCE AROUND US

Why do roots always grow downward?

No one knows exactly how, but plants are able to sense gravitational force.
The root always grows in the direction of the gravitational pull, while the shoot always grows against it. This is called 'gravitropism'.

What just happened?

The shoot of the plant will always grow against gravity. Since the carrot is actually the root of the plant, it absorbs water and transports it to the leaves. When the leaves get enough nutrition to grow, they grow against the force of gravity.

Beanstalk

Duration of Experiment: 3 days

Difficulty Level:

What you need:

Cotton

Beans

Glass jar

Water

What to do:

Step 1. Fill half the jar with cotton.

Step 2. Put the beans on the cotton against the sides such that you can see them through the jar.

Step 3. Fill the rest of the jar with cotton.

Step 4. Pour water into the jar.

Step 5. Observe the various stages of germination over the next few days.

What just happened?

Germination is the process by which plants emerge from seeds and begin to grow. The root always grows downwards, and the shoot upwards.

Carrot Top

Duration of Experiment: 14 days

Difficulty Level:

What you need:

Knife

Soil

Carrots

Dish

What to do:

Step 1. Cut half an inch off the tops (the leafy parts) of the carrots.

Step 2. Put the soil in the dish. Place the cut pieces of carrot in the bowl with the side that is cut, facing down.

Step 3. In a few days, leaves start growing on the carrot tops.

What just happened?

The carrot is actually the root of the plant. It can sustain some foliage even though it does not regenerate itself completely.

Plant Sweat

Duration of Experiment: 24 hours

Difficulty Level:

What you need:

Thread

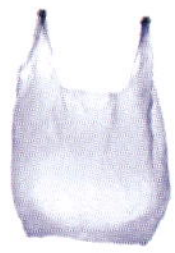

Plastic bag

Plant

What to do:

Step 1. Put the plastic bag over a few leaves of the plant.

Step 2. Use the thread to tie the mouth of the bag.

Step 3. Check on the bag the next day.

Step 4. You will notice that there are water droplets in the bag.

What just happened?

Plants lose water through their leaves in the form of water vapour, which is released in the atmosphere. This vapour condenses in the plastic bag. This process is called 'transpiration'.

Ink Prints

Duration of Experiment: 20 mins.

Difficulty Level:

What you need:

Paint tray

Paint

White paper

Rubber roller

Newspaper

Leaves

What to do:

Step 1. Use the roller to spread some paint on a paint tray.

Step 2. Place the leaf, vein side up, on a newspaper.

Step 3. Roll the paint over the leaf with the roller.

Step 4. Place the leaf, paint side facing the white paper and press it evenly. Remove the leaf to see the print.

What just happened?

The leaf is where most of the activity in the plant takes place. One can study its structure with the help of such prints.

Carbon Paper Leaf Prints

Duration of Experiment: 20 mins.

Difficulty Level:

What you need:

Leaf

Pen

Petroleum jelly

Carbon paper

White sheets

Newspaper

What to do:

Step 1. Cover the veins of the leaf with petroleum jelly.

Step 2. Place it on a newspaper and cover with carbon paper.

Step 3. Cover the carbon paper with another sheet of paper. Rub it with the smooth side of a pen.

Step 4. Place the leaf between two sheets of white paper and rub it with the pen again.

What just happened?

The carbon from the carbon paper rubs off on the leaf and creates the print.

Potato Obstacle

Duration of Experiment: 4 weeks

Difficulty Level:

What you need:

Scissors

Soil

Small toys

Shoe box

Potato (with shoots growing out of it)

What to do:

Step 1. Cut a small hole in one side of the shoe box.

Step 2. Put a little soil in the box, opposite the hole.

Step 3. Put the potato on the soil.

Step 4. Scatter the small toys around the box.

Step 5. Put the lid on and leave it on a window sill.

Step 6. Open it after four weeks. The shoot makes its way around the toys to the light.

What just happened?

Plant cells are sensitive to light and tell the plant which direction to grow in.

The Plant's Backbone

Duration of Experiment: 14 days

Difficulty Level:

What you need:

Leaves

2 tsp baking soda

Books

½ cup bleach

Bowl

Black cardboard

Water

What to do:

Step 1. Mix 2 cups of warm water and baking soda in a shallow bowl.

Step 2. Submerge the leaves in this mixture.

Step 3. Leave the bowl in a sunny area for 12 days.

Step 4. Place the leaves between 2 pages of a book and leave it for 2 days.

Step 5. Mix the bleach with 2 cups of warm water and pour the mixture into a shallow bowl till the leaves whiten.

Step 6. Dry them and mount them on a black cardboard.

Step 7. You will be able to see the veins clearly.

What just happened?

Leaves make food for the plant. The food is made in the veins of the leaf. The stem absorbs and transports the baking soda solution to the veins. When we put the leaves in bleach, all the green pigment (chlorophyll) turned white, but the baking soda in the veins didn't.

Anti-gravity Plants

Duration of Experiment: Variable

Difficulty Level:

What you need:

Seed

Soil

Pot

Water

What to do:

Step 1. Plant the seed in the pot of soil.

Step 2. Keep watering it till you see a shoot.

Step 3. Once the shoot is 4-5 inches tall, turn the plant over on its side.

Step 4. After a few weeks, the plant 'bends' and grows perpendicular to the ground!

What just happened?

Plants grow against gravity regardless of what position they are in. Changing its orientation caused the plant to change its direction of growth.

Grassy Brick

Duration of Experiment: 2 week

Difficulty Level:

What you need:

Grass seeds

Bowl

Non-glazed porous brick

Steel dish

Water

What to do:

Step 1. Soak the brick in a bowl of water for a night.

Step 2. Put the brick in the steel dish the next day.

Step 3. Sprinkle grass seeds on the brick.

Step 4. Put the dish in a sunny spot. Fill half the dish with water.

Step 5. In a few days, you will see grass sprout!

What just happened?

Though grass does not typically grow on brick since it gets no nutrition, plants are very adaptive and can survive in difficult conditions.

Raindrops

Duration of Experiment: 30 mins.

Difficulty Level:

What you need:

Glass mug

Electric kettle

What to do:

Step 1. Put the mug in the fridge for 10 minutes.

Step 2. Boil some water in the kettle.

Step 3. Hold the cold mug over the stream of hot air coming out of the kettle and watch water droplets form!

What just happened?

When water is heated, it forms vapour and rises. When it comes in contact with something cold, it forms water droplets again.

Speedy Matchsticks

Duration of Experiment: 10 mins.

Difficulty Level:

What you need:

Matchsticks

Bowl

Dishwashing liquid

Water

What to do:

Step 1. Fill the bowl with water and place a few matchsticks on the surface.

Step 2. Put a drop of dishwashing liquid in the bowl and watch the matchsticks race across the surface!

What just happened?

Soap reduces the surface tension of water, pushing the matchsticks away. The water molecules on the surface of water stick to each other, forming a sort of layer (like the type that forms on top of a soup). This is known as 'surface tension'.

Moving Molecules

Duration of Experiment: 10 mins.

Difficulty Level: ◇ ◇◇ ◇◇◇

What you need:

Eye dropper

Food colour

Glasses

Hot water

Cold water

What to do:

Step 1. Fill one glass with hot water and the other with cold water.

Step 2. Put one drop of food colour into both glasses at the same time.

Step 3. Watch as the food colour spreads faster through the hot water than the cold.

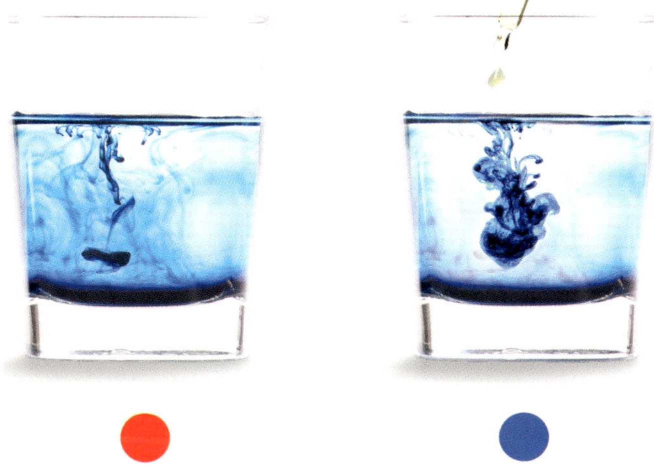

What just happened?

The molecules in the hot water move at a faster rate, spreading the food colouring faster than the cold water molecules which move slower.

Coloured Ice

Duration of Experiment: 30 mins.

Difficulty Level:

What you need:

Salt

Containers

Large tray

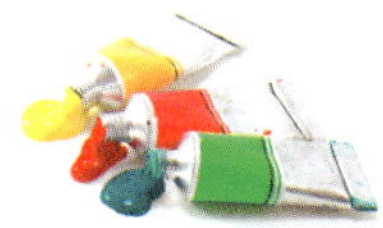
Watercolours

Water

What to do:

Step 1. Fill different sized containers with water and put them in the freezer overnight.

Step 2. The next day, take the ice out in a large tray.

Step 3. Put some salt on the ice. Wait for a few minutes.

Step 4. On top of the ice blocks, put a few drops of water colour.

Step 5. The colour runs down the ice in rivulets, creating a fantastic display of colour!

What just happened?

Salt lowers the freezing point of water. So, when you add it to ice it melts at the points where the salt comes in contact with the ice. The colour runs down the ravines made in these blocks by the salt.

Seed Balls

Duration of Experiment: 5 days

Difficulty Level:

What you need:

Seeds

Soil

Clay

What to do:

Step 1. Shape the clay into a disc.

Step 2. Sprinkle the seeds and some soil on top of the clay.

Step 3. Fold the clay inwards and roll it so that the seeds and soil get incorporated in a ball. Mould it in the shape of a hedgehog.

Step 4. Keep it in your garden. Your hedgehog will start growing spines once it rains.

What just happened?

The clay protects the seeds from wind and birds. The soil provides nutrients for them. Thus the seeds are safe till it rains and the clay soaks up the water, after which they begin to grow.

Peeling the Orange

Duration of Experiment: 5 mins.

Difficulty Level:

What you need:

2 oranges

Bowl

Water

What to do:

Step 1. Fill the bowl with water.

Step 2. Peel one of the oranges.

Step 3. Place both the oranges in the bowl.

Step 4. Contrary to what you think, the orange with the peel floats while the peeled orange sinks.

What just happened?

The peel of the orange is full of tiny air pockets that helps give it a lower density than water, making it float to the surface. Removing the peel (and all the air pockets) from the orange increases its density, making it sink. So, even though the peeled orange is lighter than the orange with the peel, it sinks.

Dry Hands

Duration of Experiment: 10 mins.

Difficulty Level:

What you need:

Coin

Talcum powder

Bowl

Water

What to do:

Step 1. Drop a coin into the bowl of water.

Step 2. Try to remove it with your hand without wetting your hand. Quite impossible, isn't it?

Step 3. Sprinkle a layer of talcum powder on the surface of the water.

Step 4. You can now put your hand in and retrieve the coin without wetting your hand!

What just happened?

As soon as you put your hand in the water, it gets covered with the powder, which makes your hand waterproof.

Wet Pepper

Duration of Experiment: 10 mins.

Difficulty Level:

What you need:

Bowl

Pepper

Water

Dishwashing liquid

What to do:

Step 1. Fill the bowl with water.

Step 2. Sprinkle some pepper onto the surface of the water.

Step 3. Dip a finger in. Nothing spectacular happens.

Step 4. Put a little dishwashing liquid on your finger and dip your finger in the water again.

Step 5. Watch the pepper race to the edge of the bowl.

What just happened?

Coating your finger with soap when you dip it in the water reduces the surface tension of the water. Therefore, the pepper spreads out.

Wind in a Bowl

Duration of Experiment: 1 hour

Difficulty Level:

What you need:

Ice tray

Bowl

Food colour

Water

What to do:

Step 1. Fill the ice tray with water. Put different food colour in each cube. Put it in the freezer.

Step 2. Fill the bowl with cold water.

Step 3. Put the ice cubes in the bowl.

Step 4. You will see coloured water around the sides of the ice cube.

What just happened?

The water that melts from the ice is colder than the water in the bowl. This means that it is denser than the rest of the water. So, it sinks.

Float or Sink?

Duration of Experiment: 5 mins.

Difficulty Level:

What you need:

Limes and lemons of about the same size

Bowl

Water

What to do:

Step 1. In a bowl of water, drop the limes and the lemons.

Step 2. You will notice that the lemons float but the limes don't!

What just happened?

Even though the lime and the lemon are exactly the same in terms of their weight and size, limes are denser than lemons. This is why the lemon floats and the lime sinks.

Rain Gauge

Duration of Experiment: 30 mins.

Difficulty Level:

What you need:

Knife

Sticky tape

Marker

Stones or pebbles

Ruler

Plastic bottle

Water

What to do:

Step 1. Cut off the top of the bottle.
Step 2. Place some stones at the bottom of the bottle.
Step 3. Turn the cut top upside down and tape it to the bottle.
Step 4. Use the ruler and marker to make a scale on the bottle.
Step 5. Pour water into the bottle till it reaches the lowest mark on the scale.
Step 6. Now put it outdoors when it starts raining.
Measure the rising water level.

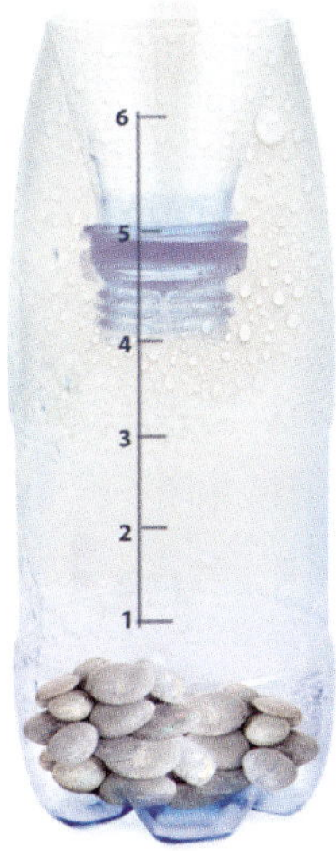

What just happened?

The rain falls on top of the gauge and collects at the bottom, where it can be measured easily. Measure the rainfall in your gauge every time it rains. Then, try to identify what type of shower it was – short or long, heavy or light.

Sweet as Sugar

Duration of Experiment: 10 mins.

Difficulty Level:

What you need:

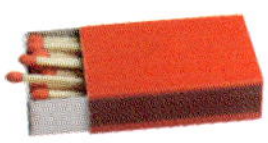
Matchsticks

Soap

Water

Sugar

Bowl

What to do:

Step 1. Arrange the matchsticks in a circle in a bowl of water.

Step 2. Touch the water in the centre with a piece of soap.

Step 3. The matchsticks drift towards the edge of the bowl.

Step 4. Replace the soap with a lump of sugar. The matches move towards the centre.

What just happened?

Sugar absorbs a little bit of water, creating an inward current. The soap reduces the surface tension of water, pushing the matchsticks away.

Crystallise

Duration of Experiment: 3 hours

Difficulty Level:

What you need:

Scissors

Black chart paper

Pan

¼ cup water

1 tbsp epsom salt (available at a pharmacy)

What to do:

Step 1. Cut the black paper so that it lines the bottom of the pan.

Step 2. Mix the epsom salt and the water.

Step 3. Pour the salty water into the pan.

Step 4. Put the pan out in the Sun.

Step 5. After a few hours, you will see lots of crystal spikes on the paper!

What just happened?

The salt dissolves in the water when you first mix it. In the Sun, the water evaporates, leaving the crystals behind.

Soap-powered Boat

Duration of Experiment: 15 mins.

Difficulty Level:

What you need:

Scissors

Visiting card

Tray

Dishwashing liquid

Water

What to do:

Step 1: Cut the card in the shape of a boat base.

Step 2: Using the scissors, make a little groove in the card at the back of the boat.

Step 3: Fill the tray with water and place the boat gently on the water, so that it floats.

Step 4: Place a drop of dishwashing liquid in the groove. Watch your boat go!

What just happened?

You broke the surface tension of water by adding a drop of dishwashing liquid. This force is enough to propel the boat.

Frozen Bubbles

Duration of Experiment: 30 mins.

Difficulty Level:

What you need:

½ cup sugar

½ cup powdered soap

Water

Bubble wand

What to do:

Step 1. Mix the powdered soap and sugar in three cups of water.

Step 2. Blow a bubble carefully in the freezer with the bubble wand.

Step 3. The bubble will soon freeze into a fragile crystal ball.

What just happened?

A majority of the bubble solution is water. When you put it in the freezer, the water freezes to form little icicles on the balloon surface.

Fireworks in a Glass

Duration of Experiment: 15 mins.

Difficulty Level:

What you need:

Fork

2 tbsp oil

Plastic container

2 drops food colour

Tall, transparent glass

Water

What to do:

Step 1. Fill the glass with water. Pour the oil in the plastic container.

Step 2. Add the food colour to the oil and mix it lightly with the fork.

Step 3. Pour the oil and colour into the glass and watch as the food colour sinks to the bottom of the glass, expanding outwards as it falls, resembling fireworks.

What just happened?

Since oil is less denser than water, it floats on top of the glass. As the coloured drops sink to the bottom, they mix with the water and diffuse outwards.

The Science of Bubbles

Duration of Experiment: 10 mins.

Difficulty Level:

What you need:

Clay

4 tbsp glycerine

4½ cups water

Toothpicks

Dishwashing liquid

What to do:

Step 1. Mix the dishwashing liquid, water and glycerine to form bubble liquid.

Step 2. Use the clay and toothpicks to make a 3D bubble wand.

Step 3. You can make a cube or a pyramid as shown.

Step 4. Dip the entire wand in the bubble mix and observe the funny shapes the bubbles make before you blow through them.

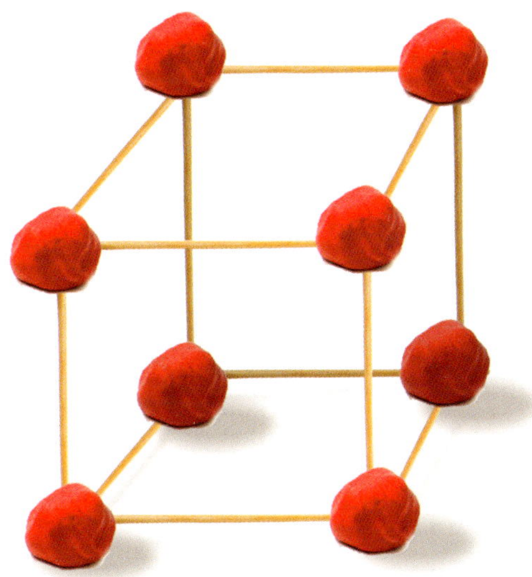

What just happened?

A bubble always tries to form a shape with minimal surface area. In free air, it is always a sphere. But with your special wand, you get an unexpected shape!

Spin the Bottle

Duration of Experiment: 30 mins.

Difficulty Level:

What you need:

Knife

3 strands of String

Scotch tape

Scissors

Bottle

Straw

Water

What to do:

Step 1. Cut the top of the bottle with the knife.

Step 2. Make six holes in the base of the bottle with the scissors.

Step 3. Cut the straw into 6 pieces and insert them into the bottle. Secure them with tape.

Step 4. Make 3 holes at the top of the bottle and tie 3 strings to this.

Step 5. Go outdoors and pour a jug of water into the bottle. Watch it spin!

What just happened?

The energy generated from the water pouring out of the holes is enough to get the bottle spinning.

Floating Paper Clip

Duration of Experiment: 5 mins.

Difficulty Level:

What you need:

1 clean paper clip

1 transparent glass of water

1 clean tissue

What to do:

Step 1. Gently drop a clean piece of tissue onto the surface of the water.

Step 2. Carefully place the paper clip on the tissue. Your hands shouldn't touch either the tissue or the water.

Step 3. Poke the tissue with a pencil and make sure that it sinks alone.

Step 4. The paperclip will continue floating on the surface.

What just happened?

The paperclip did not sink due to surface tension. Under certain conditions, surface tension helps to bind the molecules of water tightly together. This creates a platform for light weight objects and, therefore, they don't sink.

Floating Ball

Duration of Experiment: 30 mins.

Difficulty Level:

What you need:

Ping-pong ball

Plastic glass

Water

What to do:

Step 1. Fill half the glass with water.

Step 2. Try to get the ping-pong ball to float right in the middle of the glass. Tough, right?

Step 3. Now, fill the glass all the way to the top till it is almost overflowing. Voila! It is much easier to get the ping-pong ball to remain in the centre.

What just happened?

Surface tension pulls the ball towards the side when the glass is only half full, but forms a membrane for the ball to balance on when the water is filled to the brim.

Invisible Fire Extinguisher

Duration of Experiment: 10 mins.

Difficulty Level:

What you need:

Cup

Matchsticks

4 tsp baking soda

2 tsp cooking vinegar

Candle

What to do:

Step 1. Mix the baking soda and vinegar in the cup.

Step 2. Let the mixture stop fizzing and light the candle.

Step 3. Pretend that there is a liquid in the glass and 'pour' it over the candle to magically snuff the flame out!

What just happened?

The baking soda and vinegar reacted to form carbon dioxide. Fire needs oxygen to burn. When you 'poured' the carbon dioxide onto the flame, the flame did not get any oxygen and so it died.

Drinkable Density

Duration of Experiment: 10 mins.

Difficulty Level:

What you need:

Pomegranate juice

Orange juice

White grape juice

Eye dropper

Glass

What to do:

Step 1. Pour the white grape juice in the glass.

Step 2. Use the eye dropper to drop the orange juice on top of it.

Step 3. Finally, drop the pomegranate juice on top.

What just happened?

The juices are of different densities because of the differing amounts of sugar dissolved in them. White grape juice has the most sugar, and pomegranate juice, the least.

Sundial

Duration of Experiment: 12 hours

Difficulty Level:

What you need:

Stick

Watch

What to do:

Step 1. Fix the stick vertically into the ground.

Step 2. Every hour, mark where the shadow of the stick is falling. Number the marking depending on the time.

Step 3. To see the time, just look at the shadow and read the corresponding number.

What just happened?

The shadow of the stick depends upon the position of the sun, which changes every hour.

Spilt Oil

Duration of Experiment: 15 mins.

Difficulty Level:

What you need:

Food colour

Tub

Oil

Water

Rubber bath toy

What to do:

Step 1. Fill half the tub with water.

Step 2. Add blue food colour.

Step 3. Put the small toy in the tub.

Step 4. Pour the cooking oil into the tub. Swirl the mixture to create waves.

Step 5. Notice how the oil and water don't mix, but your toy gets coated with oil.

What just happened?

Oil is not as dense as water and doesn't mix with it. This is exactly what happens during oil spills when marine life gets effected by it.

Tornado in a Bottle

Duration of Experiment: 10 days

Difficulty Level:

What you need:

Glitter

Glass jar

Water

Dishwashing liquid

What to do:

Step 1. Fill 3/4th of the glass jar with water.

Step 2. Add a few drops of dishwashing liquid and some glitter.

Step 3. Put the cap on tightly.

Step 4. Quickly spin the bottle in a circular motion for a few seconds.

Step 5. Stop and look inside to see if you can see a mini tornado forming in the water.

What just happened?

Spinning the bottle in a circular motion creates a water vortex that looks like a mini tornado because of a force called the 'centripetal' force.

Grow Bacteria

Duration of Experiment: 3 days.

Difficulty Level:

What you need:

Petri dish

Gelatine

Ear buds

Newspaper

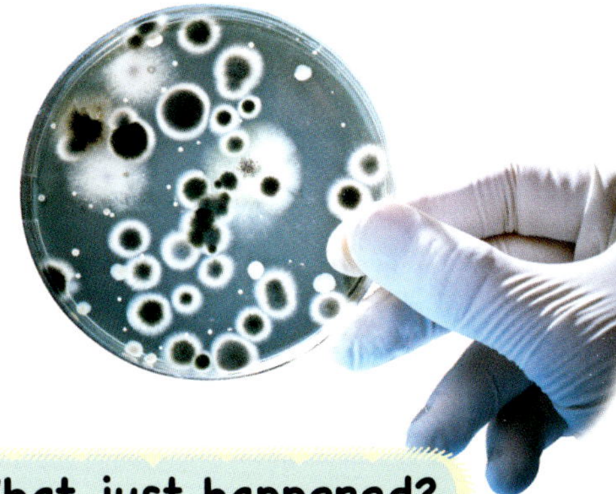

What to do:

Step 1. Make a gelatine solution in the Petri dish. Let it solidify.

Step 2. Collect dust from your house on a ear bud.

Step 3. Rub it on the Petri dish and put the lid on it.

Step 4. Keep the dish in a warm area for 3 days.

Step 5. Check the dish to see the growth of bacteria.

Step 6. Dispose the dish by wrapping it in newspaper and throwing it in the bin.

What just happened?

Soft, moist and warm conditions are ideal for the growth of bacteria.

Bread Spores

Duration of Experiment: 2 days.

Difficulty Level:

What you need:

Bread

Ziplock bag

Milk carton

5 drops of water

Rubber gloves

! Be careful while handling the mould and don't smell it.

What to do:

Step 1. Put water on the bread.

Step 2. Seal the bread in the ziplock bag and put it in the milk carton. Wear rubber gloves while handling the bread.

Step 3. Open it after two days to see mould spores of various colours and textures.

What just happened?

Spores develop into living fungus when the conditions are suitable, such as on the damp bread.

OTHER TITLES IN THIS SERIES